Book Description

Literacy is one of man's most treasured possessions. From the dawn of time, we have wanted to mark our history in mud, clay, and stone. Reading is such a valuable, treasured possession that it was once reserved for kings, clergy, and noblemen. With reading comes knowledge and knowledge is power. Even in the digital age where reading takes place less often on paper and more on technological devices, it is still as important as ever. Take, for example, the humble e-reader, a simple device with a memory and a screen, not actually much more advanced than an LCD calculator; it can literally store a library's worth of books, all accessible at the touch of a button. But what good is all of this information available to us on websites, social media, and reading devices if we do not possess the basic skill of reading and retaining what we read?

"Speed Reading Techniques: Practical ways to improve reading speed and increase comprehension, read faster and understand more", is an all-encompassing guide on reading quickly and understanding all that you read. Written and compiled by an expert in the field, the book is sure to allow the reader to develop the speed reading and comprehension skills they need or desire. Aimed at a wide audience of varying reading skill levels, *Speed Reading Techniques: Practical Ways to Improve Reading Speed and Increase Comprehension, Read Faster and Understand More* enables the novice, less-experienced reader, to improve their overall reading speed and comprehension, allowing them to enjoy reading and perhaps even develop a love for the hobby. More advanced readers such as academics who find this book will enable them to further increase their reading rate and overall retention of the content read. In addition to general readers and academics, the book provides a guide on reading a multitude of literary styles including fiction, newspapers, and technical manuals. With a host of tips and tricks as well as daily practices and a place to record your progress, *Speed Reading Techniques* is everything anyone needs to be a better reader and have fun doing it.

This begins with a basic introduction to speed reading, what it is and why it is helpful or even necessary to some. Everyone is a potential speed reader and one of the first things the book tackles is what holds you back from reading quickly and retaining all the information that you have read. Some challenges to speed reading include, but are not limited to regression, whereby the reader goes back and reads the same word or paragraph over and over again. Subvocalization is another challenge that is addressed; explaining why we read under our breath or with moving lips and how to stop doing just that. It further addresses the physical factors involved in reading such as our focal range, how much our eyes can take in at one time, teaching the reader how to increase this range and be able to see more at once. In order to address all of these challenges, the book provides us with multiple corrective practices, assisting the reader in increasing their reading rate overall as well as their comprehension and content retention rate.

Not all literature is created equal, and as such, different literary styles require different methods for maximum reading speed, comprehension, and content retention. We focus on some of the most commonly encountered reading material including newspapers and technical and scientific guides, providing specific methods for reading each most effectively.

Speed Reading Techniques

Practical ways to improve reading speed and increase comprehension. Read faster and understand more

Rick Bishop

attempting any techniques outlined in this book.

By reading this document, the reader agrees that under no circumstances is the author responsible for any losses, direct or indirect, that are incurred as a result of the use of the information contained within this document, including, but not limited to, errors, omissions, or inaccuracies.

Table of Contents

Introduction

Have you ever found yourself in a situation with limited time and far too much information to pore over? Perhaps you are a student, and like many of us, you have procrastinated before a big quiz or exam to find that you have one night to absorb a semester's worth of material. Perhaps you are an executive and have piles of essential paperwork to go through before another one of your numerous meetings. Alternatively, you could simply be one of those that enjoys catching up with recent news, a good novel, or some juicy tabloid story, and you have limited time to spend reading during your busy day.

Speed reading in itself can help you get over the time limitations that we all encounter during the fast-paced lifestyle in this day and age. However, speed reading alone cannot help you to assimilate and process the information you read over. In this e-book, we will cover how to assess your reading speed and improve on it with practice sessions that you can do daily to help build your skill and comprehend and absorb the information you are reading over.

As an evolutionary trait, humans have learned to adapt to making fast [sometimes life-saving] decisions based on the information they receive in the blink of an eye. Think of how quickly you react as you notice a basketball hurtling toward your head. In a split second, a multitude of internal processes happen. Your eyes see the basketball racing toward you and they send a message toward your brain. Your brain is able to take that information in, process the data, and deduce that the object racing toward you will be painful should it strike you. The brain then calculates the time until impact and what options are available to avoid that impact. Based on this information, the brain can calculate the best course of action which could include you dodging out of the way, ducking down so that the basketball misses you, or possibly even raising your arms to protect your face or to swat the ball out of the way. The same can be said for the way our brains multitask, take in information, and make deductions based on information while driving. When you are cruising down the highway, your brain is taking in the information around it from inside and outside the vehicle such as what speed we are traveling at, how much fuel is available, using your gears, following the course set out for you, changing lanes, taking turns when needed, and watching for other cars and hazards on the road. While all of this information is imperative to your safety, you will probably find yourself singing along to the radio, keeping up a conversation with a passenger, or even thinking about what you feel like making for dinner.

How is it possible for our brains to take in, process, and make decisions based on that amount of information, and yet when we focus on reading a paragraph, it's possible not to recall or comprehend what we have just read? The answer, it seems, lies in how we as humans are taught how to read from a young age. Children are taught to see the letters in front of them and correspond them to a sound. For instance, the combination of the letters C-A-T sounds different from the letters C-A-U-G-H-T simply because of the way the letters sound when they are corresponding. The combination of these letters gives us different words, and word associations give us different meanings. When the terms "hot" and "dog" are combined, we know that it could either mean that the dog's temperature is elevated or they could refer to a delicious treat. Context is essential for our brain to identify which meaning we need to associate with those words. Visually, your brain can comprehend information much faster in a picture than when the information is given to you in a text - as an example, the fifth Harry Potter book, "The Order of the Phoenix," is more than 200 000 words. Yet, the same story is told in the movie, which is less than 2h 30min. The question posed to us then, is why do we read so slowly when our brains have the ability to process information with such speed? The answer to this is quite simple: Our brains read each word in a sentence one...at...a...time. Thankfully, this is something we can learn to overcome, and the chapters in this book will help you train your brain to do just that, increasing your reading speed and comprehension as you go.

Many myths surround the process of speed reading. Dating back to the 1950s, many scientists have come up with ways to improve the way humans read and understand a text, hoping to aid the absorption and comprehension of knowledge. Even though speed reading is a widely sought after skill, many people still feel that speed reading is just "skim reading." Skim or scan reading happens when an individual rapidly glances through a piece of text, looking for certain words or phrases to stand out - clues as to what they are looking for. This process is useful for individuals looking for specific information in a body of text, rather than understanding the entire body as we will help you understand how to achieve.

As we live in a society where time-saving and digital presence is at the forefront of our evolution, there are many applications around today that promise (albeit mythically) to increase your speed reading exponentially. Many of these applications use a process which eliminates the movement of the eyes called saccades. Saccades refer to the side to side or jerking movements that the eyes make in order to read words in a sentence. While this process does limit the need for the eyes to move to relay the information to the brain, unfortunately, this does not teach your eyes to read faster. When words are flashing on a screen in the same position, it's effortless for your brain to take in the "picture" it creates and to understand the meaning. When a person then tries to read that fast in a normal context, the eyes still need to move over the sentence, which means that they revert to the speed that they initially did. Even though your rate "increases" as you work through these exercises, they do not help individuals with the core issue of reading through and understanding a body of text in its traditional format.

Acquiring the ability to speed read will bring numerous positive aspects to your life. The first positive influence is the psychological advantage to learning a new skill. As humans, the same way that we feel more powerful and self-confident when we go from walking to jogging to running, our brains benefit from the challenge of learning a new skill and overcoming the goals we set for it. Self-confidence can also be achieved because once we have read and understood instructions or concepts, we feel more in control of the situation, information, and knowledge, making us feel adequately prepared to use that information efficiently without needing to revert to double-checking on what we have read.

An obvious benefit that we gain from learning to speed read is the time we save every day. The same principles apply when we are reading the morning newspaper, skimming the tabloid for interesting information about our favorite celebrities or wading through pages and pages of research material. If we learn to read faster, and with more comprehension, we will minimize the time we spend stopping to ponder the piece. As stated above, we will not need to go back over the information to 'catch" something that we might have missed. Speed reading also boosts our concentration and focus. When you learn to control the way you read, you will find yourself more focused on the topic at hand, remembering important points and minimizing the cognitive "clutter" we experience when our mind wanders as we read through the text. Information retention becomes more natural and more important as we concentrate more efficiently. Being able to quickly understand how to assemble or operate machinery, devices, or software or to smoothly and efficiently sift through reports is imperative to help you in your career or help you get ahead of your competition.

One of the more surprising benefits of learning to speed read is the enjoyment of reading a good book or novel that some individuals experience. Many people simply do not enjoy reading as a leisure activity because it becomes frustrating and time-draining. Some individuals feel that they miss certain important information as their mind wanders while reading through chapters or the process of reading simply takes too long. In a world where instant gratification is no longer a luxury but rather a priority, learning to speed read through a novel is a skill that many individuals should be investing their time in learning.

To set achievable goals as you move forward in the following chapters, aim to increase about one hundred (100) WPM (words per minute). If you feel this is too heavy as you work through it, change the goal to fifty (50) WPM. Keep checking your progress using the methods above and keep a diary of how you are progressing to chart your progress. Remember - the goal is not merely to skim over the text as fast as you possibly can. The primary purpose of learning to speed read is to increase your comprehension of the text without falling into old bad habits.

PART 1: FIVE RULES OF SPEED READING

Chapter 1: Resist Regression

At one point or another, all of us have struggled to read a novel or body of text while tired or distracted. This leads to our mind wandering and results in what is commonly referred to as "reading on auto-pilot" for a large amount of time. This means that although we have gone through the motions and mechanisms of reading, we have not absorbed anything that we have gone over. Once we realize this, we go back and reread the passage or text over and over again until we understand it.

While there are some exceptions to this, rereading text isn't always a good habit to pick up. Not only does it waste time while reading and mean that we do not absorb the text we have read, but it also frustrates a reader. When this happens, many of us stop trying to read, put down the book or papers, and sometimes never go back to them. This also affects the self-confidence of the reader, making them believe that either they are not cut out for this reading activity or the book or text is a "difficult read" which leads people to dismiss it.

The human brain is much more intelligent than most people give it credit for. It's an efficient machine that also works to conserve energy. Like most people who are incredibly smart, the brain always tries to find the fastest and easiest way to fulfill a task. If you introduce the belief in your brain that you can go back at any time and read the information again, the brain will not utilize the process for absorbing the information. Instead, it is aware that you can go back and fact check the instructions or information as and when you need it. For example, let us look at the process of preparing a frozen meal with specific reheating instructions. You take the box out of the freezer, look over the instructions, and think to yourself "this sounds easy, it's a simple process." You remove the food from the box and throw the box in the bin. You get through the first instruction and poke small holes in the cellophane cover and pop it in the microwave. Suddenly you can't remember how many minutes you need to microwave the food, so you grab the box out of the bin and reread the instructions. This happens to me at least once every time I heat up a ready-made meal and at least five times every time I cook from a set out recipe. The brain's process of efficiency is great for conserving space for memory and energy, but it is a horrible way to save time. It has an inherent laziness and tends toward the quickest way to get the job done. This is why, for centuries, many of the world's civilizations have a belief in brain exercises whether they be in the form of prayer or meditation. These exercises focus on clearing the "clutter" from the brain, improving focus and concentration.

One thing to remember, however, is that there is a difference between rereading and regressive reading. Rereading a section can be helpful when you are trying to learn a subject or instruction. Rereading happens when we complete a section and then skim through the text, reminding ourselves of the important points and highlights. We should make sure to read through a full section before going back to reread. Regressive reading or "regression" is when we allow our eyes to travel backward in a sentence or passage. As discussed in the introduction, eye movements, or saccades, are very important when we are attempting to speed read. We need to limit the movements our eyes make when they are going over text in order to read in a smooth, rapid way. When we allow our eyes to regress, it breaks the flow of the passage as well as our concentration. Sentences are constructed in a very specific way in any language. This is called syntax, the arrangement of words and phrases to create well-formed sentences in a language. The syntax is arranged so that the reader may be able to read swiftly and with comprehension as quickly as possible. When we allow our eyes to wander back over the sentence, we break the natural syntax of a sentence. When our brain does not recognize the natural flow of a sentence as we have been taught from the day we learned to read, the brain needs to stop and decode the meaning of that sentence. When this happens, not only do we waste precious time trying to understand what should be fairly easy for the brain to comprehend, we also disrupt the thinking process of the brain - instead of understanding the context of the sentence, the brain is caught up understanding how the sentence works.

Thankfully, there are many ways for us to limit the habit of regressive reading. The first step is to be conscious of the fact that we do this. Read over the following passage, an excerpt from *Lord of the Flies* by William Golding, and keep a mental note of every time you jumped backward in a sentence:

The shore was fledged with palm trees. These stood or leaned or reclined against the light and their green feathers were a hundred feet up in the air. The ground beneath them was a bank covered with coarse grass, torn everywhere by the upheavals of fallen trees, scattered with decaying coconuts and palm saplings. Behind this was the darkness of the forest proper and the open space of the scar. Ralph stood, one hand against a grey trunk, and screwed up his eyes against the shimmering water. Out there, perhaps a mile away, the white surf flinked on a coral reef, and beyond that the open sea was dark blue. Within the irregular arc of coral the lagoon was still as a mountain lake — blue of all shades and shadowy green and purple. The beach between the palm terrace and the water was a thin stick, endless apparently, for to Ralph's left the perspectives of palm and beach and water drew to a point at infinity; and always, almost visible, was the heat.

As you can see, regressive reading may be a problem that we have and do not realize that we are even doing it. The first step to getting rid of any bad habit is the acknowledgment and consciousness of the fact that we have a bad habit. Then comes the decision that we would like to change the habit in order to grow or get better at a skill. Speed reading is a skill like any other. If you want to run faster, there are bad habits that you need to acknowledge such as the incorrect breathing, gait, and your focus. Your brain, eyes, and other systems associated with reading (whether it be fast or slowly) are workable systems that humans can train over time. For some people, it is easier to overcome these patterns that break our concentration and our productivity, for some it will be harder to unlearn and relearn how to read effectively and efficiently. Some of you may not even find that you regress during your reading as much as others, but your mind simply wanders and you need to reread what you have already been over. This is also a form of reading regression and we can combat this using the steps listed below as well. Whether we do it out of a lack of self confidence in our reading skills, out of a lack of focus on the job at hand or we have become distracted by our thoughts or surroundings, these practices to help curb reading regression will boost our ability to learn to speed read and help us to become much better at analyzing and sifting through material (or simply help us to enjoy the pure thrill of reading through a good book).

Backwards regression is not the only concern when we are looking at the issues that hinder us from reading more efficiently. We sometimes also encounter issues such as "forward regression" and of course distraction. Remember, one of the main issues for those learning to speed read is the eye movements, and they don't always move backwards. Forward regression occurs when our eyes skip over the words we are currently reading and land on words or sentences that should occur later. The main problem with forward regression is just as the name suggests, we then come to realize what happened and we go back to the previous sentence. This becomes an issue as our eyes are trained to move mostly either left to right or right to left. For those who were taught to read in languages like English that reads left to right, simple scanning exercises work much better when we scan our eyes left to right. Examples of this are word searches or scanning for targets or patterns in a game like "Where's Waldo." For those who learned to read in languages such as Arabic or Hebrew, the opposite will be true, they will spot patterns and targets in a right to left motion quickly. So, when we go against our natural inclination of sideways movement, the eye loses its place very quickly and the rhythm of reading is lost. In the case of distraction, the reader's eyes catch on words above or below what you are reading. Mostly, this happens when a reader has a certain list of words in their mind to look out for when reading through material. Subconsciously, the brain is scanning the peripherals for those words and when it notices them, it locks on to one of those significant words. This becomes an issue because not only are your eyes moving incorrectly in a sideways motion, but they are also jumping up and down. This is one of the easiest ways to get lost in a body of text.

Practices to Help Overcome Regressive Reading:

The methods for the daily practices are interchangeable and you should determine which of them works for you. For instance, if you find yourself reading regressively because your eyes go back to previous parts of the text, you should focus on the white paper practice. If you find that your eyes get regressed forward further than the words surrounding the sentence you are reading, the pointer method could work for you. If you find that pacing and peripheral words are what is distracting you, the tracker and pacer method may be beneficial. The key to finding out what practice is best for you is to try all of them and see what yields the greatest growth for you as a reader.

All of these practice methods should employ the same basic principles as outlined below:

1. Set aside a minimum of thirty minutes (30) each day to follow these practices.
2. Firstly, you must make a conscious decision to focus and concentrate on the passage which you are reading or learning. Take a few deep breaths before you begin, clearing your mind of clutter and abstract thoughts. This is extremely important as you begin to learn speed reading.

Eventually, it will become a positive habit as you progress with the skill. As with any skill, the will to overcome our bad habits and relearn positive ones is always the first step. Consciously deciding that you are going to make a concerted effort to focus and concentrate will take you a lot further than you will believe.

3. Try not to surround yourself with distractions. Many students, for instance, will play their favorite music in the background when they are trying to study. This is an extremely distracting practice and will make it harder for your brain to focus on the task at hand. When you play catchy music in the background, your mind is subconsciously tracking the music and lyrics even if you are not aware of it. A nice quiet room, especially when you are going through your daily practice sessions, will do wonders for your focus and attention. In the next section on subvocalization, we will discuss what type of music you can play in order to help you concentrate on what you are reading.

4. PUT YOUR PHONE AWAY. In today's culture, it is easy to fall into the trap of always being connected, but our brains are so tuned into the sound of an instant message or notification that it will pull you away from your goal. Setting your phone on silent is good, but it is even better to leave it in another room (on silent in another room is even better so you don't hear notifications). If you are reading on your

phone or tablet, make sure to put it into "do not disturb" mode so you won't see the notifications and turn the brightness on your screen down to minimize overload of your eyes. Advise your friend or family that you are not to be disturbed for x amount of time as well to be able to give your brain the time it needs to focus on the task.

5. Start off your regression training practices with a book or text that is easy to read, not crucial (not something that you need to study or report on) and pleasant - no daily news pieces that might make you upset or anxious. You want to make the experience a good one, something that you will enjoy reading.

Practice 1: Using a page to block out the previous text

This practice is specifically to stop you from rereading sections of the text that you have already read over. The practice centers on training your eyes not to go back and moving the page away so you can do that should be discouraged completely.

1. Get yourself a plain, white sheet of paper that you cannot see words through, yet is easy to move either up and down your screen or up and down the pages of a book. This part of the exercise is better done when working with the written

word in a book as it is easier to see through a white page when your screen is bright. It is also easier to fold a piece of paper over your page and move it up and down. During these times, though, most of our literature comes in a digital format, so if you are using a e-reader, tablet, smartphone, or something similar, make sure to turn your brightness down as stated in point number two.

2. As you read through one line of text, move the plain white paper down to cover that line. Keep doing this as you go. This acts to focus your brain on the line just under the white page, and stops you from being able to look back and reread the previous line. It also minimizes the problem of getting lost in the text you are trying to read.

3. If you find that you feel like you haven't understood what you have read, push on. You should always resist the urge to pull the paper back to reread a sentence or section. The aim here is to push you into reading continuously and not regressing back to previous points, especially if you are reading a piece from a novel, many parts of the text are not essential to your understanding of the story. They either describe characters, situations, locations, or visual scene setters. Many textbooks also reiterate points later on in the text, or provide examples, so you may understand it better at the end. If you really feel like you have missed something, run through the exercise again, using the sheet of paper as you did before. Most of the time, by the time you get to the

end of the piece you will find that you have understood more than you thought while you were reading once your brain has had a chance to process the information.

Practice 2: Using the "Pointer Method"

This practice method was designed by Evelyn Nielsen Wood, a school teacher in Utah in the 1950s. Evelyn boasted that she was able to read at a remarkable 2700 words per minute (WPM) by using her finger to guide her eyes. This became known as the pointer method, and is also sometimes called "hand pacing" or "meta guiding."

1. As you read through the body of your selected text, use your finger to sweep along the line as you read.
2. Your eyes should follow your finger, reading the words that appear behind it and only those words.
3. Make sure to move your finger at a comfortable pace, adjusting the speed up or down, depending on how you are reading and absorbing the text.
4. Try to increase the speed consciously every few sessions and monitor whether or not your reading is keeping up with the increase in speed.

Practice 3: Using the "Tracker and Pacer Method"

This is a practice involving using an object to bring your attention to the words you are reading. It is similar to the "pointer method" as it centers around training your eyes to follow a certain pattern, distracting you from the need to dart your eyes back and forth across the text. It makes use of the normally negative peripheral distractions of the eyes to train them to stay on course.

1. Find yourself a pen with a cap on it, or something similar that will act as a "pointer."
2. Underline or "track" under the line as you read through it, making sure that your eyes do not deviate from the words above the pen.
3. Increase the speed of the pen every few sessions and you should start to see a change in the pace at which you read.

As an interesting note on Practice 2 and 3 above, many above average readers use similar methods while working on a PC. When we type up and read over reports or stories, it is easy to miss certain errors, because our brain remembers what the sentence should say and edits it in our mind. Of course, no one wants to waste time, especially on a deadline, so they speed read through the work they have just completed. Many will use either a variation of the pointer method, highlighting the words as they go along, or a variation of the tracker and pacer method, using their cursor or mouse pointer to run along under the sentences.

Chapter 2: Minimize Subvocalization

When we are children, the act of learning to read is both an exciting prospect where we can make all the words that swim in front of us make sense and also a daunting task as those same words seem to trip us up as we learn new phrases and how their meaning could change depending on how they are grouped together. It is a very specialized course that teachers need to go on to make sure that children have a good solid basis upon which to learn and grow, seeing as every subject and every field of study requires at least a basic understanding of language and comprehension ability to be taught. Many centuries ago, the written word was a luxury only afforded to the higher economic classes and the middle class where it was necessary for them in their occupation. Lower class families worked menial jobs and had no need to learn to read or write as their jobs did not require it. In today's age, almost every form of occupation requires the ability to read and write. From being a graduate to writing out our resumes to filling in job application forms, the vast majority of jobs need these abilities. Especially as we live in a digital age, the ability to use more complex machinery and software is a must - not only to get you a job to begin with, but to give you an edge over competitors for advancement.

When we are first taught how to read when we are children, the lessons are very basic with the premise being to sound out the word. Teachers will start children out with the letters of the alphabet, giving them the phonetic sound of the letter before moving on toward the correct name for each letter. Basic words are given, usually around the 3 letter count with the standard C-A-T, D-O-G, etc. Once young learners have mastered the simple pronunciations of letter combinations, they are fed increasingly more difficult letter combinations, some which look like they should be pronounced one way, but with rules about the letter combinations to help us put them into the correct parts of our brains. Think of "I before E except after C." Of course, there are always exceptions, but many of us still remember these little sing-song rules from our childhood. Especially when it comes to writing, many of these deeply ingrained rituals come back to us. Even as I sit here writing this, I sometimes refer back to my early years when I try to spell more complex words. The problem with this technique is that sometimes our brain mixes the skills of writing with the skills of reading. Since we were taught to sound out words that we could not pronounce to understand what the word is and what it means, sometimes, as we read, we still find ourselves doing this. Subvocalization refers to the act of actually sounding out the words that we read. There are different degrees that people do this, but in all cases, there is always a time wasting element that we hope to minimize with the skill of speed reading.

The degrees of subvocalization:

1. <u>Physically sounding out the words as we read.</u> For some people, reading is a difficult task, especially when you are not a native speaker of the language you are reading. Many people will pronounce the words aloud or under their breath. This limits the speed at which we read to a greater degree as the pace at which we read becomes slower even than the pace at which we speak, as not only are we stopping on every word to read it out, but we also need to hear it as we say it and process that before moving on to the next word.

2. <u>Mouthing out the words silently as we read.</u> Some people will simply move their mouth as they read words. Although it is not as bad as physically saying the word, as we don't need to hear the word to comprehend it, the act of moving our mouth does slow down the process of reading to sub-talking speed.

3. <u>Silently reading the passage to ourselves.</u> When we are taught to read, we are taught to read out loud. Once we were fluent enough, we were probably taught to say the words in our heads. Although it does not waste as much time as either moving our lips with the words or saying them out loud, we are still relying on the auditory aspect of reading to comprehend a sentence. Even by hearing the words in your own mind, we limit ourselves based on the fact that if

we can't pronounce a word in our head, we get stuck on that particular word, bringing down our overall reading speed and disrupting the flow of our eye movements.

Most readers who do the first and second form of subvocalization are aware of it and know that they need to change their habit. It's the third form of subvocalization that trips most people up. It feels natural to be reading the words in your head as you go through a sentence as that is how we were taught. Many people who read novels will even attach accents to the words they are reading depending on the context and environment that the writer has given them. For the purpose of this book, however, we are not trying to set a scene in a narrative. We are trying to learn the skill of speed reading to be able to get through large pieces of text quickly and efficiently. While subvocalization is effective when reading poetry or flowery imaginative pieces, it does little for your speed reading ability, oftentimes actively slowing us down.

Below is an excerpt for you to read through from The Wonderful Wizard of Oz by L. Frank Baum. While you are reading through it, try to pick up what form of subvocalization you are using.

"Oh, dear! oh, dear!" cried Dorothy, clasping her hands together in dismay; "the house must have fallen on her. Whatever shall we do?"

"There is nothing to be done," said the little woman, calmly.

"But who was she?" asked Dorothy.

"She was the wicked Witch of the East, as I said," answered the little woman. "She has held all the Munchkins in bondage for many years, making them slave for her night and day. Now they are all set free, and are grateful to you for the favour."

"Who are the Munchkins?" enquired Dorothy.

"They are the people who live in this land of the East, where the wicked Witch ruled."

"Are you a Munchkin?" asked Dorothy.

"No; but I am their friend, although I live in the land of the North. When they saw the Witch of the East was dead the Munchkins sent a swift messenger to me, and I came at once. I am the Witch of the North."

"Oh, gracious!" cried Dorothy; "are you a real witch?"

"Yes, indeed;" answered the little woman. "But I am a good witch, and the people love me. I am not as powerful as the wicked Witch was who ruled here, or I should have set the people free myself."

"But I thought all witches were wicked," said the girl, who was half frightened at facing a real witch.

"Oh, no; that is a great mistake. There were only four witches in all the Land of Oz, and two of them, those who live in the North and the South, are good witches. I know this is true, for I am one of them myself, and cannot be mistaken. Those who dwelt in the East and the West were, indeed, wicked witches; but now that you have killed one of them, there is but one wicked Witch in all the Land of Oz-the one who lives in the West."

As you read through the passage, did you say the words out loud? Did your mouth move with the words? Or did you simply read the words to yourself in your head? Generally, it comes as quite a shock to most of us that we are reading to ourselves in our heads. Many of you may even come to this point and ask how it is possible to read through without the narrative in your mind. It is indeed possible to visually see and understand words without needing to say them in your head. For example, when you see the letters U-S-A, you immediately associate them with the country The United States of America without needing to vocalize them. The same applies when you see a "STOP" sign while you are driving. You do not say "stop" in your head, but your brain recognizes the word, understands it, and takes the action of what needs to be done. Most people also do this with numbers in a sequence. When you read the number 6,952,634,184, you can tell by looking at it, that it is a large number. Most people will subconsciously count the numbers after the first and recognize that it is in the billions and work back from there. You don't need to read the number as 'six billion, nine hundred and fifty two million, six hundred and thirty four thousand one hundred and eighty four.' Your brain will automatically recognize what the number represents. In context, a "number sentence" does not need to be vocalized in your mind. 3 x 2 gives you the automatic answer of 6 without you needing to hear it in your mind. This is because our language and mathematical teachings were different from the beginning. Imagine how much easier it would have been to study science and biology in school without vocalizing the complicated and often difficult to pronounce scientific words for elements and compounds? When we can see the word, "australopithecus," as a visual word and not need to stop and think of how to pronounce it, we would read through these texts much quicker without getting stuck.

Reading is not about the words you see, rather the information that you gain. Many of the words in sentences are there for grammatical understanding such as "is," "and," "a," and "at." You do not need these words to be able to understand the knowledge, context or information that you will gather from that sentence. When you focus solely on the words, you are focusing on sentence construction and grammar, rather than the idea of what it is trying to tell you. This is why "parrot" learning is so ineffective in studying. When students are given textbooks to learn from, very rarely do examiners ask them for direct quotes. Students are given scenarios in order to assess their level of understanding of the subject, and not the textbook definition. For example, when mathematics or science students are given a formulae or a law to study, they are not asked to quote it in examinations, but rather to apply it to situations or problems given to them.

It is extremely difficult to unlearn something that has taken root in our lives from an early age. These habits of subvocalization have been the basis on which we learned to read from the days of "Jack throws the ball." We will start with the first degree and work our way through to the rest of the habits of subvocalization.

First Degree of Subvocalization: Physically Saying the Words as You Read Them

This one is an elementary process of elimination and a good starting point, especially for non-native speakers. The fix for this type of subvocalization is to simply keep your mouth closed and not emit any sounds. It may seem simple, but when you have been doing it all your life, it could be tricky to stop yourself from saying the words out loud. Try to stop yourself from mumbling the words or making sounds while reading. With a bit of practice doing this, you will see your reading speed jump quite quickly.

Second Degree of Subvocalization: Moving Your Lips as You Read

Even though you might not be saying the words out loud, moving your lips will also slow your reading process. This is because your mouth moves slower than your eyes, thus limiting the potential to learn how to move your eyes faster over text. To combat this bad habit, there are two effective solutions. The first is to put a pen or a pencil across your mouth as you read. Hold it in place with your lips. This will stop your lips from being able to move without dropping the pen or pencil. When you have mastered the art of holding the pen or pencil in place, pop a stick of gum into your mouth. As you are chewing the gum, your mouth is preoccupied with the motion and will not concentrate as much on the forming of words while you are reading. You will still have to focus on not forming the words with your mouth, but the motion of chewing will help to distract you from doing this.

Third Degree of Subvocalization: Internally Reading the Words in Your Mind

By far, this is the hardest subvocalization to completely eradicate. You might not even be able to get rid of this habit entirely. The key here would be to try to minimize the instances as much as possible, suppressing the need to read to yourself in your head, and hopefully this reduces the dependency on doing it at all. While you are learning to get rid of this habit, you may notice some overall comprehension of the words may elude you. This is why it is important to practice these techniques on pieces that are not crucial to you and definitely not something you are attempting to learn or analyze until you are more comfortable with the techniques as we have outlined. Internally subvocalizing the text has most likely been the way your brain has understood text for many years, so focus rather on minimizing the internal conversation and the techniques first before you test them out in real world applications.

Our brains are wonderful processing machines. The left hemisphere is the side that deals with our reading ability, and while it's a complex hemisphere, it is also a serial processing system which means that it can only deal with the information it receives on a linear one-to-one basis. The right hemisphere is the one that trips us up with subvocalization. The right hemisphere deals with all things creative and abstract, such as audio and art. For your brain to be effective, it needs to engage both hemispheres, but both your hemispheres are not built for speed. That is why so many of these practices deal with a mechanism of distraction.

Do not be concerned if parts of your brain try to tell you that if you are not hearing the voice inside your head, that you are merely skimming and not reading the piece. Remember, reading is not the act of going through every... single... word... Reading is simply absorbing information and knowledge about the piece that you are going through. Our brains

Some of the techniques below will help you to distract your brain from vocalizing the words you are reading in your head:

1. Chewing gum: As mentioned before, chewing gum can help distract your mouth from forming the words as you read, but if you concentrate on the motion of chewing, your brain becomes more occupied without needing to read through every word. That being said, you have to actively concentrate on the motion. Our brains are wired in such a way that motor skills like those involved in chewing and eating (something we have done our whole lives to be able to survive) can continue in an unobscured way while we have other mental tasks at hand. The brain has been proven to be able to effectively enact two tasks at once, but not three. This is because we have two hemispheres of the brain, and the brain halves the tasks and delegates the tasks to one of the hemispheres. Once we add a third task to the mix, the brain struggles to cope as there are too many mental pathways to work through and it is not as efficient as it is prone to be. The reason that we can eat, talk and perform another task is because the eating side is taken care of in the motor skills section and not a process that we need to think about. This is also why a process like breathing is completely autonomous, yet used in many meditation practices to clear your mind. When you focus on the act of breathing in and out, many other unconscious processes like our minds wandering or stressful thoughts are deferred from in our brains.

2. Listening to the right kind of music: Similar to chewing gum, listening to the correct type of music can have the same effect. While we urge you to stay away from trending music that your brain will lock on to, the effect of listening to an instrumental music such as classical music, nature sounds, or something similar can have a positive effect on concentration and distraction from subvocalization. Sounds that seem to ebb and flow engage the audio section of our brain that can mean the necessity to "hear" the words we read fall away. Again, it's important to keep a slight focus on the music as we learn to get rid of the dependency of hearing the words we read. For those who would like to understand the science of why this works, as stated previously, the left hemisphere of the brain is involved in the processing of information and the right hemisphere is involved in the more abstract. So, your left brain hemisphere deals with lyrics in music, and your right hemisphere deals with the melody of the song. While trying to read, your left brain hemisphere is already engaged in processing information while your right brain hemisphere needs to be engaged. This is why subvocalizing text [while being slow] is effective in retaining information. By giving the right brain hemisphere something to listen to as a melody and without lyrics, it effectively distracts that part of your brain and allows your left brain hemisphere to concentrate on the information it is receiving from the text,

also allowing you to accelerate your reading speed (because you are not only reading at your speaking speed) and retain more information.

3. "Chunking:" At some point of your practices of suppressing your inner subvocalization, you will find that you cannot completely eradicate the need to hear your inner voice. This is where "chunking" comes in to help you. Instead of focusing your brain on each word in a sentence as you read it, try to form "chunks" of words to concentrate on. As we have said previously, not every word in a sentence is essential to the comprehension of the passage. In the art of chunking, we group words up and only effectively let our inner subvocalization pronounce one of those words. It does not necessarily need to be the first word in a chunk, but the most important word. For instance, "Jack and Jill went up the hill." When you read that sentence, you do not need to focus on all the words. If you chunk them you may just see "Jack," "Jill" and "hill." the idea is the same, yet your brain is not processing words such as "and."

4. Another method for chunking is to read over the chunks over words so fast that it is difficult for the speech section of your brain to keep up. It is perhaps impossible for humans to actively say more than one word at a time, which means that when you visually chunk words together, your inner voice cannot pronounce it. When you read "knowledge is power" you will probably say all three words

separately in your mind as "knowledge-is-power." however if you combine it together, you will not be able to say "knowledgeispower" at once, even though you recognize the words as you read them. As you move your eyes over chunks of words very fast, your brain cannot "pronounce" them in your head, which means you could not hear them in your mind.

5. Word distraction: Word distraction has also become increasingly popular as a form of distraction. This practice is currently one of the top solutions for minimizing subvocalization, although it does require a bit more practice to work effectively. The practice hinges on the idea that you hear something else in your head as you are reading and not the words in front of your eyes. Eventually, you will not need the word distraction and you will be able to read without it so that you can read a lot faster and not have your mind preoccupied (this is when your comprehension levels will go up as well). Word distraction can come in two forms. First of all, you can simply say one word over and over in your head while you are reading. Choosing which word you use is up to you. You can start off with something complicated like "aluminum" with multiple syllables to truly distract your mind from pronouncing the words you are reading. As you begin to feel comfortable doing this, you may want to change the word to something with a single syllable which is very simple like "cat." This helps in two

ways. One, you will begin to not think about the word as much while you are reading, focusing your concentration on the material rather than the word as it does not require much concentration to repeat. Secondly, the faster repetition of the word will aid you in gearing up your reading speed. You can start to say the word faster and faster to get a faster rhythm going. You can also use a counting method for this practice. Instead of using one word repetitively, you can count as you read. Generally counting from one to three is the accepted practice, as it is quick and easy. Again, you can also start to speed up the tempo of your counting as you get more comfortable. Using the counting method may help you to focus on groups of words rather than each individual word.

6. Forcing your eye movements to be faster: If you can force your eyes to move faster over a piece of text than they normally would, eventually the frontal cortex of the brain where our speech centers are will not be able to keep up. Your brain will begin to only subvocalize some of the words and you will ultimately stop hearing those words as you read through.

Percussion exercises can also play a part in helping to minimize subvocalization. As discussed, instrumental music can play a part in helping to distract the brain from pronouncing words in your mind as you read. Percussion can

46

also help with this. Percussion basically means striking one object with another in order to produce a sound. Percussion instruments are used to keep a beat. In this context, we will guide you through some ways you can use percussion to control and limit your subvocalization, but first, let us look at why percussion can be useful to you.

If your brain is focusing on a steady beat, it is unlikely to be focusing on the act of hearing your inner voice pronounce the words you are reading. Increasing the tempo at which you use percussion can also aid you in reading faster. This reinforces the point that the faster you read, the less likely it will be that your brain will be able to pick up and pronounce the words as fast as you are reading them.

Practices for Percussion:

1. Using a metronome: A metronome is an object or instrument used in music to help musicians to keep a beat as it gives a specific "click" to indicate timing and tempo. The advantage to using a metronome is it's consistency. When you set it to a specific BPM (beats per minute) you can be sure that it will keep to that rhythm. As you attempt to learn to read faster, you can increase the speed of the beats per minute. However, most metronomes can only

reach a speed of around 250 BPM (beats per minute). A speed of 250 WPM (words per minute) is already the average reading speed, which means that this could be beneficial to slow readers keeping tempo of words as they go over them, but for average to advanced readers, you may want to move the tempo to beats per line depending on what medium you are reading in.

2. Using your hand: It is also possible to use your hand to beat a steady rhythm on, for example, your thigh or a table. The tempo is inconsistent, but the sound of the tapping combined with the feeling of your hand hitting your thigh will distract you enough that the "voice" should be minimized in your head.

3. Using a pen or pencil: This is a useful technique that can be helpful to you, but fairly annoying or distracting to others, so take care if you are using this around family or friends or in places like a library or study hall. How many times have you noticed someone tapping a pen or pencil while reading? This form of distracted action has been around for quite some time, although many people would probably not even understand why they are doing it. It is effective because of the sharp sound it generates.

4. In a pinch: If you either find yourself in a situation where you have no "instruments" around to use, or are in a public setting where you cannot make a noise while reading, there are small "quick fixes" you can employ to get the job done.

Though not as effective maybe, they will work in the short term. You can either tap your teeth together (with your mouth closed) or tap your tongue against the roof of your mouth. These are not recommended for an extended period of time, and be sure not to tap your teeth together too hard or you might damage them.

Chapter 3: Expand Your Focal Range And Use It More Effectively

We touched briefly in the introduction and one of the previous chapters on your eye movements during the reading process. This chapter serves to expand that subject and explain why our eyes move the way they do, how we can optimize the movements, and how to train your eyes to move more efficiently to aid us in reading faster.

In the late 19th century, French ophthalmologist Louis Émile Javal described the eye's movements during reading as the "visual processing of written text." He reported that eyes do not move continuously along a line of text, but make short, rapid movements (saccades) intermingled with short stops (fixations). The early observations that he made about eye movements during the process of reading involved watching people read with the naked eye. Toward the end of the 19th century and into the 20th century, researchers began creating technology that would map out the movement of the eyes over a piece of text, primarily to learn how people read, how it affected human behavior, and what the most effective form of reading was to help students especially to learn better. One of the main advancements was that of non-invasive technology to map out the human eye movements across written text which thereby helped to trace the cognitive behavior (the process of thinking, attention, memory usage etc.) associated with the way we read and how the human brain processes the information. Leonardo Da Vinci pioneered some of the existing theories on cognitive behavior we now find in modern research as far back as the 14th century. Da Vinci was fascinated with the human eye movement. He did a lot of his research on "optical modelling" based on dissections of the human eye which he then used to model water-filled crystal balls. His main research was framed around where exactly in the human eye the most attention and clarity came from. His research helped us to understand the difference between focal points and peripheral areas of sight. Focal vision is the dead-on vision associated with looking straight at an object. This vision is clear and takes in all the available information on what is being seen. Peripheral vision is the information that your eye sees around the focal point. Because of the conical shape of the human eye, our peripheral vision contains "blind spots" which means that we sometimes miss crucial information. The reason that we don't continuously see black or "blind" areas as we look around is because our brains are efficient enough to "fill in" the missing information, usually in the form of blurry colors, so our vision appears to be uninterrupted. I'm sure, if you have ever learned to drive, you are aware that blind spots can be problematic as you may not see hazards on the road or other vehicles attempting to overtake you (especially smaller vehicles such as motorcycles, cyclists, etc.). This is why we are taught to move our heads before changing lanes, to make sure that we check these blind spots to avoid a collision.

There are two important movements to consider when dealing with the movements of the human eye. The first is saccades. Saccades are the small, quick "jerking" movements of the eye as it goes through text. To illustrate how your eyes move saccadically when reading a line of text, close one eye. Gently place a fingertip over your eyelid and read a few lines of text with your open eye. You should start to feel how your closed eye moves through the text. When we read a passage, our eyes do not naturally move smoothly through the text. As we read through a line, the eyes dart forward, then forward again, the forward again. It's generally thought that other than blinking, saccades are the fastest movement produced by the human body.

Smooth movement of the eye is generally quite slow, so the quick, jerking movements actually aid your reading to be able to move quicker over text and not to strain your eyes too much. You may notice, when you have a lot of information to take in visually, your eyes "dart" around processing as much information as possible because of the movement of the focal point back and forth. You will also notice that your eyes do not dart in a linear motion but rather back and forth, up and down, etc. This is so that your brain can also process the information in your blind spots. Saccades also do not happen in torsion (the clockwise or anticlockwise movements) unless you consciously make them do it - torsion requires greater stress on your eye muscles, fatiguing them very quickly. Saccades work with the amygdala, a component in your brain of the limbic system (which controls emotion and behavior). The amygdala was thought to only control basic functions such as the "fight or flight" response, but has recently been shown to actually control more of our responses to emotion. The connection between the amygdala and the saccadic movements of our eyes is apparent when someone is in a vulnerable or potentially threatening situation. For example, when a person is in a situation where they feel fear, like 3 to 4 people approaching them in a dark alley, the eyes will move rapidly, scanning the positions of the people, possible escape routes and hazards in those escape routes. Is there a door close by that they could run through? Is there a lock on the fence just behind assailant number 3? Are the more assailants that I don't see straight away? Are there potential onlookers who may come to my aid? Are any of them carrying weapons? Do I think I could possibly fight my way out of this situation? All of these questions are answered by the information the eyes take in and the information needs to come through very quickly in order for self-preservation to kick in. The amygdala then needs to swiftly formulate a response to the question: "do I run or do I defend myself?" Similarly, as we interact with other human beings, the saccadic movements of our eyes help us to determine clues about the other person. If someone cannot make eye contact, they are restless, they are maybe sweating or wringing their hands, they are potentially lying to you. There are very small clues we learn to pick up from an early age about human intent and the visual clues we pick up from our eyes darting around are invaluable to reading other human beings. With regards to reading, the saccadic movement of our eyes allows us to read faster with less eye strain. The average reader's saccadic movement can be between 200-250 m/s (meters per second) whereas a reader with advanced reading speed may go up to 500 m/s. Information has shown that advanced readers' saccades are longer than the average, resulting in them taking in more information before their eyes rest on a fixation point.

The next movement to consider is that of fixation points. Fixation or visual fixation means that one is maintaining the visual gaze on a single location. This means that as your eyes are engaged in saccadic movement, there are points where it stops (albeit briefly) and either carries on in its movement as in the case of reading or darts in another direction as explained above. Fixation, in the act of fixating, is the point between any two saccades during which the eyes are relatively stationary and virtually all visual input occurs. During saccadic movement, the eyes are not taking in more peripheral information than focal.

The tiny amount of time where your eyes stop between saccades is where you process the focal information in that spot.

During the process of reading, your eyes will use both these operations. The eye muscles will jerk across the text (saccadic movement) and stop on random words in a sentence (fixation points), resting for 0.25 seconds or 250 milliseconds. Sometimes, readers fixate on letters as opposed to whole words. It is believed that a reader can take in a span of about seven to nine letters to the right of the fixation and three to four letters to the left before it jumps over to the next fixation point, assuming that you are reading in a language that writes left to right. The opposite would be true of a reader reading a piece of text written in a language like Hebrew or Arabic where writing is done from right to left. You read more letters in the direction which your eyes are tracking. An average reader will have fixation points every two (2) or three (3) words. In a speed reader, the fixation points can sometimes be up to six (6) words at a time, or in extreme cases, one every sentence. Although it seems like a trick in reading where you almost "skim" words and make up your own conclusion based off of the letters that you concentrate or fixate on, this could not be further from the truth. Speed reading is not the art of skimming text, but rather training your brain to take in the information in a much faster and more efficient way, by identifying the habits that limit your ability, training yourself to change them and working on making your brain more efficient at processing the same information in a faster way. Even when working with fixation points and saccadic eye movement, the brain is still seeing and processing all the letters in a sentence. We are just training our eyes to rest less or training our brains to have less fixation points and working the peripheral part of the process more. This is why speed readers can read efficiently and still be able to tell the difference between words that are similar in letters, yet are completely different words such as spatial and partial, principal and principle, grill and girl and so on. The eyes see the words, the brain processes the words, but because we do not need to rest our eyes on every word in a sentence, it does not slow us down. This is the same reason that we try to minimize subvocalization. When we don't have to pronounce every single word in a sentence, we do not need to fixate on every single word, thus reducing the time we take to get through a body of text.

Practices to Train Your Eyes to Read Faster

Training Your Eyes to Use Fixation Points More Effectively.

Most average readers will find that their saccades unconsciously move in such a way that their fixations fall on the first and last words in a sentence. This is a waste of your peripheral vision. When doing this, you are actually wasting your peripheral vision on the margins of the text that contain no information at all. In the exercise below, we will give you a passage to read from Harry Potter and the Prisoner of Azkaban by J K Rowling. Try to pick up where your eyes end up fixating:

Aunt Marge was Uncle Vernon's sister. Even though she was not a blood relative of Harry's (whose mother had been Aunt Petunia's sister), he had been forced to call her "Aunt" all his life. Aunt Marge lived in the country, in a house with a large garden, where she bred bulldogs. She didn't often stay at Privet Drive, because she couldn't bear to leave her precious dogs, but each of her visits stood out horribly vividly in Harry's mind. At Dudley's fifth birthday party, Aunt Marge had whacked Harry around the shins with her walking stick to stop him from beating Dudley at musical statues. A few years later, she had turned up at Christmas with a computerized robot for Dudley and a box of dog biscuits for Harry. On her last visit, the year before Harry started at Hogwarts, Harry had accidentally trodden on the tail of her favorite dog. Ripper had chased Harry out into the garden and up a tree, and Aunt Marge had refused to call him off until past midnight. The memory of this incident still brought tears of laughter to Dudley's eyes.

-   Excerpt from Harry Potter and the Prisoner of Azkaban - J K Rowling © 1999 by J. K. Rowling

Can you see where your eye movements are fixating? Below is the same piece, but the areas where you should train your fixations to happen are underlined:

Aunt Marge <u>was</u> Uncle Vernon's sister. <u>Even</u> though she was not a blood <u>relative</u> of Harry's (whose mother <u>had</u> been Aunt Petunia's sister), <u>he</u> had been forced to call her "<u>Aunt</u>" all his life. Aunt Marge <u>lived</u> in the country, in a house <u>with</u> a large garden, where she <u>bred</u> bulldogs. She didn't often <u>stay</u> at Privet Drive, because <u>she</u> couldn't bear to leave her precious <u>dogs</u>, but each of her visits <u>stood</u> out horribly vividly in <u>Harry's</u> mind. At Dudley's fifth <u>birthday</u> party, Aunt Marge had <u>whacked</u> Harry around the shins <u>with</u> her walking stick to stop *him from beating Dudley at musical statues. A few years later, she had turned up at Christmas with a computerized robot for Dudley and a box of dog biscuits for Harry. On her last visit, the year before Harry started at Hogwarts, Harry had accidentally trodden on the tail of her favorite dog. Ripper had chased Harry out into the garden and up a tree, and Aunt Marge had refused to call him off until past midnight. The memory of this incident still brought tears of laughter to Dudley's eyes.*

Your fixations should be placed about three (3) words from the beginning of a sentence, in the middle and about three (3) words from the end of the sentence. This allows your peripheral vision to take care of reading the rest of the sentence, without being wasted in the margins of the text. Of course, in smaller textual mediums such as newspaper articles, the middle fixation is not necessary due to the contracted nature of the paragraph.

Training Your Eye Muscles to Move More Freely

Because your eyes are controlled by six muscles that you use every day, the chances that you are even aware of them are quite slim. However, like any muscle, just because you use them every day does not mean that you cannot strain them. By doing some stretching exercises, you can expand your focal range in order to be able to move them faster - like a runner stretching their muscles in order to run faster. The more flexible your eye muscles are, the more you can make use of your peripheral vision.

- Sit in a comfortable position, with your eyes fixed on a point straight ahead of you.
- Lift your right arm out to your side, in line with your shoulder.
- Point your right thumb up toward the ceiling.
- Slowly move your eyes to the right, as far as you can until you can see your thumb clearly.
- Take care not to strain your eye muscle too much, or you could hurt it.
- If you cannot see your thumb clearly, bring your arm toward the center until you can.
- Mentally take note of where your arm is positioned - each time you do this, you want your arm to be a little further back, until it is straight out along your side.
- Gently bring your eyes back to the center and repeat the exercise with the left arm and left eye.
- Practice this a few times, at least once a day alternating between the left and right arm and eye.

- Up and down motions are not necessary for reading, but if you feel like you would like to stretch those muscles as well, incorporate stretching your eyes to look up at your eyebrows, then back to center. Then stretch them down toward your lower eyelids. Make sure not to squint your eyes if you do this or you could encounter some discomfort.

*Note: please take care not to push your eyes too hard or you will strain the muscles around the eye. Like any muscle that becomes strained, this could take a few days to heal properly.

Eye Writing

Training your eye movements in ways that they don't naturally move is also a good way to stretch out those muscles. As mentioned before, our eyes don't naturally move in a curved motion unless we are tracking something specific. Eye writing is effective in getting our eyes "out of their comfort zone."

- Sit in a comfortable position, with your eyes fixed on a plain wall on the other side of the room to you (or the furthest possible wall).
- You would want to choose a wall that does not have objects hanging from it or anything that may distract you.
- Move your eyes slowly and deliberately and spell out your name with only your eye movements (imagine your eyes

were like a paintbrush and you were spelling out the letters of your name).

- Make sure not to move your head.
- Eventually, move on to wringing out the alphabet in small letters (a, b, c, d, e, etc.) as the curved nature of the smaller letters will be more beneficial for this exercise.
- Take care not to squint your eyes while attempting this exercise as this may cause discomfort.

What to do if Your Eyes Feel Strained

Eventually, sometime during either these exercises or while you are speed reading through a novel, you will encounter some form of eye strain. This may manifest in your eyes "jumping" or tearing up, or even a burning sensation as if they are dry. You may even feel that the muscles around the eye feel a little tender, or at the very worst develop a sort of headache that feels like it is sitting just above or behind the eyes. This is eye strain and unfortunately, in a world driven by many screened devices, it is all too common. Eye strain can also occur if you are tired and attempting to read through a body of text or study for an examination.

Thankfully, there are tips to be able to alleviate the discomfort and sometimes outright pain of eye strain:

1. Rest your eyes. Sometimes the best remedy for tired strained eyes is to close them. Taking naps or going to sleep seems to help the most, but of course, it's not always a viable option if you are at work, in a meeting, or in a class.

2. Hooded eyes. Almost as good as closing them completely is to shut them halfway. This relaxes the muscles around the eyes and limits light and visual input from straining them more. As you shut them halfway, you will notice the eyes tremble slightly. To stop this, you can focus on a faraway object and they should stop trembling.

3. Eye Squeezes. Eye Squeezes stretch out your muscles and promote blood flow back into not only your eye muscles, but your facial muscles as a whole (as a side note, be careful when doing this in public as it may cause some alarm to onlookers). If you feel the need to yawn while doing this exercise, do so. Yawning also promotes more oxygen intake, while stretching out your face muscles.

A. As you inhale deeply and slowly, open your mouth and eyes as wide as possible

B. As you exhale slowly, squeeze your eye muscles tightly as well as screwing up all the muscles in your face as much as you can.

C. Hold your breath for about 10-30 seconds, while still squeezing all your facial muscles tightly.

D. Relax your facial muscles and breathe in again.

E. Repeat the steps a few more times (about 5 times in total).

Chapter 4: Increase Comprehension and Memory

Now that you have learned how fast you currently read, how regression is holding you back from reading faster, how subvocalization is a bad habit and how to get rid of it, and how to train your eyes to move faster, we move on to the most important step in speed reading - how to increase your comprehension of the text and remember it all later. After all, there's no point in being able to read fast if you keep having to go back over text again and again to remember it, is there? When you first begin to increase your reading speed, it's natural to feel like you're not absorbing the information as effectively as you once did. That is why, as you go through the practice sessions, you should not worry about your comprehension as much. The first step is learning to process the text quickly. Once you have that solid foundation, you can build on that to absorb the information and remember it.

Getting Into the Correct Mindset

Whether you are under pressure to get a work assignment done, you need to study for an exam, or you're just short on time, the expectation in the modern world is that you need to be performing at 110% capacity at all times. This pressure and stress places a huge burden on our minds and, in turn, that places more of a burden on our cognitive ability.

1. Before you begin with learning to absorb and retain information from a body of text, take a few deep relaxing breaths.

2. Try to focus your mind on the task at hand. What are you reading? What information are you hoping to gain from the text? What is the desired outcome of the task? Are you learning a subject or merely reading through an article or novel? Are you looking for key words of phrases to deduce information?

3. Before you begin to read, especially when you are learning a subject or looking for information, read the table of contents and take note of the flow of the book or subject matter. Some of the information may not be critical to your task (such as examples, anecdotes, history), so you can worry less about retaining that particular information.

4. Make sure your eyes are rested and ready for the task. You may want to try some of the relaxation exercises we outlined in the last chapter to make sure you can take full advantage of your eye movements, you know where your fixation points should be and you are ready for the task.

5. Organize the space around you. If you need to make notes,

have a notebook and pen handy. If you take notes on your tablet or laptop, make sure to turn off all your notifications. These just serve to distract our mind from what we are attempting to achieve.

6. Have a drink of water, coffee, tea, etc. available to you so that you do not have to break your concentration and flow if you feel thirsty.

7. Take breaks regularly. As students, we were taught to take breaks from studying for a good reason. Use your breaks effectively. Do not switch on the television as this will distract your mind from what you have been learning. Physical activities like going on a walk or playing with a dog will promote blood flow and increase oxygen, helping our brains to not become tired and fatigued.

Memory

Memories can be tricky. The main purpose of memory in the human brain is to store information over a period of time. Once a memory is created, the brain must store it somewhere. How that information gets stored in your brain depends on how you perceive it. First off, we have sensory memory - textures, visual memory and sound. This type of memory lasts only a brief moment. It is, however, possible to recall these memories at a later stage depending on the memory. For instance, you may be able to recall the texture of a teddy bear or the weight of your smartphone yet you might struggle to remember the color of a car you saw if you were not paying attention. The sensory memories that we can recall are usually classed as "familiar" memories, something that either brings you comfort or lets you know that something is wrong. This is something we may encounter when we pick up a bag, for instance, and feel that there is weight missing, we immediately know that we have forgotten or lost something.

The next type of memory is short term memory. Short term memory is limited in its capacity, and cannot recall more than around seven (7) items at a time. For instance, if you try to remember a long number of say ten (10) digits - 5003264852 - you may struggle to remember it flawlessly. Yet, we can remember telephone numbers with relative ease. Why is this? When we break the number into chunks of information, we will have better memory recall - 500- 326- 4852 - That is a lot easier to remember than a sequence of 10 numbers!

What we are attempting to learn here, however, is how to convert the information that we take in to long term memory, our third and best type of memory. Although all of the kinds of memory we possess are important, the long term memory is the one that we often struggle with, especially when we want to use the information later. Unlike short term and sensory memory, which is limited, our long term memory is more reliable and unlimited in time and capacity. A human brain does not have a limited amount of data available, unlike computers. It's really only age (slowing down of brain neurons), brain damage or deterioration and diseases such as Alzheimer's and dementia that can erode our memory.

We often hear people say that they do not have a great memory. This is not entirely true, as the brain does not have a limited capacity. It's rather that some people have an issue with converting short term memories into long term memories. Let's look at an example: I am sure that most (if not all) of you reading this can remember at least some of the words to your school's song, or at the very least, your country's national anthem. In most cases, this was something that was taught many years ago, but through repetition and practice, you are able to recall the words and melody with very little prompting. However, we may not know where we put our smartphone, keys, glasses or wallet if we have not put it in the same place as usual. This is because we were not focused when we set these items down. When you actively make a note of where you have set something down, you are converting that memory into something you will need later, thus making it so that you are able to recall the information.

Memorization of Information

Below are practices and techniques in order to help you get better at converting the information which you are reading into long term memory:

1. Focus on what you are reading. When the mind is distracted, it does not see the information as important and therefore will discard it.
2. Be present. When you are taking in information as if you are listening to an important lecture being given on the subject, your mind will automatically pay more attention.
3. Use acronyms. One of the oldest tricks at school is to use acronyms to remember important sequences and lists. I'm sure many of you still recall the little rhymes from school, the likes of "Betty Eats Cakes And Uncle Sells Eggs" to spell "because" or PEMDAS from mathematics to remember the order of operations (Parentheses, Exponents, Multiplication, Division, Addition, Subtraction) or the order of the planets from "My Very Exhausted Mother Just Served Us Noodles" (Mercury, Venus, Earth, Mars, Jupiter, Saturn, Uranus, Neptune). Acronyms are invaluable, although many people dismiss them as childlike.
4. Acrostics. Similar to acronyms, acrostics use a sequence of letters, mostly A, B, C, etc. to aid our memory. Unlike

acronyms, acrostics bridges sentences or thoughts together. Traditionally these are used to form passages or poems from a word (usually someone's name), but you can reverse that procedure and use it to remember the sequence of words in a passage:

Out, out brief candle!

Life's but a walking shadow, a poor player,

That struts and frets his hour upon the stage

— MACBETH, ACT 5 SCENE 5, LINES 23-25; MACBETH TO SEYTON

Or make up your own memorization of a subject

Three (3) main things affecting air pressure:

Temperature of the Air

Altitude or Elevation

Moisture present in the air

5. Create associations to other subjects. When we create associations in our brain, we create more neural pathways to that information. The brain can recall information quicker when we have more neural pathways relating to the

70

subject, especially if we create associations to information we know more about. For instance, if you understand how computers store and use information, associating short term memory to RAM (Random Access Memory) and long term memory to ROM (Read Only Memory), you would understand these processes easier and be able to recall them better later.

6. Repetition. There are two forms of repetition that work to increase our memory in different circumstances. The first is audible or written repetition. When we take notes, we are already starting to remember something better. There isn't a need to copy it down word for word as this takes us back to "parrot learning" which we know does not work effectively. Try to write the information down in a different way or in your own words. Another method is to, in an audible sense, try to verbalize the information to yourself or another by describing the information differently to someone else as if you are teaching them. The next form of repetition is to do exercises involving the information. If it is studying that you are concentrating on, find some examples of old exercises or test papers and go through them, using the information that you have just gone through. The more you use the information you have learned, the easier it will be to recall how to do it again in the future.

7. Visualize the information. When we are creating neural

pathways to information, a visual representation can work wonders for our memory. As we discussed in one of the previous chapters, our brain reacts much quicker to a visual prompt than to the written word. Whether you visualize a setting from a novel, create a picture of a formula or sequence of information, or simply visualize how a process works that you are learning about, you create more information for your brain to store. As they say, "a picture is worth a thousand words..."

8. Mind maps. Another form of the visualization of information is to create a mind map. A mind map mimics the way the brain stores information in neurons, with sub information that branches off. The mind map needs to be concise and to the point, with key words and memory prompts, rather than long and difficult to recall. The use of color will also help to fix the picture in your mind.

9. Give the information a story. When we try to remember mundane facts, our brain tends to be bored. If you find yourself needing to remember "boring" facts, dramatize a story for them. For instance, to remember the chemical composition of water (H_2O), think of two Hydrogen twin atoms trying to court the same Oxygen atom. The more ridiculous or dramatic the story, the more inclined you would be to remember it.

10. Use scent. Because our memories need to go through the first two memory phases in order to be converted to long

term, try to boost the first process by attaching a smell to the memories you begin creating. Rosemary has often been considered to be one of the best scent boosts to our memory. While you are studying or taking in information, try to keep some sort of scent near you that will be enough for you to notice, but not overwhelming. For an added boost, if possible, try to take some of that scent with you into an examination, for instance, as a little reminder of the first process of building the memory.

11. Name Image Associations. While remembering names in particular, it's a difficult process. Most people will remember faces or details of a person's appearance a lot easier than their name. You can use distinctive parts of the subject's appearance, however, you may not see a picture of someone in an examination, so therefore, associating one's name with a fact about them would be a better option. For instance, when learning the inventor of the telephone's name is Alexander Graham Bell, you could associate the sound of a telephone to that of a bell.

12. Utilizing your breaks effectively. As we mentioned before, you should be taking regular breaks while going through material. However, if we distract ourselves too much while doing this, we could stop the process of converting the information to long term memory. When we take breaks, we should try to take a walk, breathe fresh air, etc., but also think back on the information that you have covered. This

does not mean that you need to quiz yourself on the information, rather, think about it in a practical sense, use the time to develop the associations to other information, think of clever, funny ways that it could be useful or ways that could help you to remember it. All of this is building extra pathways in our brains to access that information.

13. Chaining. Use silly or funny scenarios in your head to remember a sequence. For instance, if you need to remember how many miles are in a kilometer (1.60934): one old man made a point of eating six hotdogs on an empty (ZERO) stomach to impress the lady dressed to the nines while her three brothers for(four)warned her.

14. Memory Palace. Memory palaces have been documented as one of the favorite ways to remember information. It's a tricky process to learn, but if you start off simple and use it more, it will become a very strong technique that may help you to be able to remember almost anything. The basic principle is this: create an imaginary palace in your mind. Most people also use a familiar setting such as their school or home. As you learn information, visualize putting it into your palace. These can be sequences of things or just general things in no particular order. An example of a memory palace would be to remember the colors of the spectrum in order (or the colors of a rainbow):

Picture yourself walking through the door of your palace, a

bright RED door. As you walk down the hallway, the first room you encounter is painted ORANGE, with an orange balloon inside. You walk further down and see a YELLOW room with a big bouquet of sunflowers inside. The next room down the hall is GREEN with big tropical plants all over. The next room is a BLUE bathroom with the water running into the bath. The next room is INDIGO with many huge bird cages with indigo colored birds flying around. The last room down the passage is VIOLET and a little girl in a violet sundress is eating purple cotton candy.

There are many different ways to convert your short term memory into long term memories and going through these practices will help you considerably. They are also dependent on the type of information you need to remember, be it sequences, processes or just a chunk of information. It's up to you to decide which of these practices will work best for you and the content which you are reviewing.

Chapter 5: Daily Practices and Recording Progress

In order to work through the chapters, you will need to be able to track your progress. In this chapter, we will concentrate on how to track your reading speed and comprehension using all of the topics that we have covered.

In order to track your progression of words per minute (you should be re-evaluating this every day as you go through these exercises), we refer back to the section on how to calculate your WPM (words per minute):

Method 1

1. Copy a substantial amount of text into a word processor (e.g. Microsoft Word). Be sure to choose something that you might encounter in your daily life, something harder may take you longer to read through.
2. Set a timer for one (1) minute.
3. Read the text at a pace that is comfortable while you are able to comprehend and remember the information.
4. When the timer goes off, highlight the text from where you

stopped to where you began.

5. The amount of words you read in that minute will be your WPM (words per minute).

Method 2: For Physical Print Books

1. Choose a piece of writing as above - something that you would be able to read easily and smoothly.

2. Set a timer for five (5) minutes.

3. Read the text at a pace that is comfortable while you are able to comprehend and remember the information.

4. When the timer goes off, mark the spot where you stopped with a small pencil mark.

5. Count the number of words in the first five (5) lines.

6. Divide the number of words by five (5). This gives you the average words per line.

7. Count the number of lines you read from the beginning to your pencil mark.

8. Multiply the number of lines you read by the average words per line (as you calculated in step six (6). This is how many words you read over the five (5) minute period.

9. Divide this number by five (5). That is your WPM (words per minute)

*If you would like an more accurate average, try both methods. You should find that they both fall into the same range of WPM (words per minute).

To have an idea on where your current speed falls as a general rule, refer to the table below:

1 – 100 wpm	Children learn to read at this reading speed. This is borderline literacy. There is little understanding and recollection of material read. Reading is very hard work in this range.
100 – 200 wpm	This is below average and this person typically does not enjoy reading. It is difficult to read and stay up to date and learn. This person's comprehension is below 50%.
200 – 250 wpm	Most likely, your reading speed falls in this range. This is the average person's reading speed. But you are re reading words and subvocalizing words and comprehending only about 50% of what you read.
250 – 350 wpm	This is slightly above average range and most likely a post high school graduate but the comprehension still is a little more than 50%.

350 – 500 wpm	This range is well above the average reading speed and probably someone that enjoys reading. The retention is good and usually 50-75%. This is a very good reading speed.
500 – 800 wpm	This is a very respectable and incredible reading speed. You obviously really enjoy reading and few fall into this high reading speed category. You definitely like the book better than the movie :)
800 – 1000 wpm	This is a very efficient reading speed. At this reading speed you have no stress or pressure about reading. You understand words and their meaning very easily and probably have had some form of speed reading training. You don't re read words and rarely subvocalize words.
1000 wpm & faster	Wow – awesome! Reading at this speed you have complete control over reading and have mastered. This is an elite reading category. Reading is a huge part of your life and you have complete control over everything in regards to reading.

*table taken from https://memorise.org/speed-reading/calculate-reading-speed

You should find yourself a pleasant novel to read though for your daily exercises, one that is within your language ability (not one that is a "hard read" for you). Novels will keep the same writing style, tempo and give you enough text to comfortably read through around thirty (30) minutes each day without running out of story.

Each day, you should attempt one of the techniques from each chapter. This is so that you can see if any particular technique helps you more than others. If you find one technique is helping you more than others, continue to use that one so your reading skills can improve.

For the purpose of the chart below, you should list the following:

WPM - This is the words per minute that you will calculate each day when you are done with your exercises

REGRESSION - List the technique you used to combat reading regression each day here.

SUBVOCALIZATION - List the technique you used to minimize subvocalization here.

EYE MOVEMENTS - List the eye movement exercises you have used here (remember to note if your fixation points are improving).

MEMORY TOOLS - List the memory tools you have used here. Also score a 1 to 5 rating on how you feel you have comprehended the text by the end of it, with 1 being not at all and 5 being completely.

COMMENTS - Here, you can make comments on the practices as you have felt they work for you. If there is something you are struggling with, something you feel like you need to try tomorrow or if you have found a technique that you believe has been extremely beneficial to you.

Remember to go through your daily practices first, then use them as you calculate your words per minute (WPM) at the end of your practices.

Before you begin your daily practices, make a note of your base WPM here: _____

Where would you like to be at eventually? _____

DAY #	WPM	REGRESSION	SUB-VOCALIZATION	EYE MOVEMENTS	MEMORY	COMMENTS
Day 1						
Day 2						

Day 3						
Day 4						
Day 5						
Day 6						
Day 7						
Day 8						
Day 9						
Day 10						
Day 11						
Day 12						
Day 13						
Day 14						
Day 15						

Day 16						
Day 17						
Day 18						
Day 19						
Day 20						
Day 21						
Day 22						
Day 23						
Day 24						
Day 25						
Day 26						
Day 27						
Day 28						

PART 2: DIFFERENT APPROACHES AND TECHNIQUES FOR REVIEWING LITERATURE

Chapter 6: Newspapers

Far back into our history, before the written word took over, the only way to get caught up on what was happening around us was to go to the town square and listen to the town crier tell us what was happening. Town criers were important for two reasons, they were the only way to consolidate the information being received from travelers from other towns and cities for the people of the area (without the age old "broken telephone" which meant that information changed slightly each time it was told, resulting in the information getting fragmented or simply falsely reported). The second important job of the town crier was to let the people know important information coming through from their king, government, or parliament. Without this important information being relayed to the people, there would be many miscommunications and the people would not know what was happening around them.

In Venice, around the 1500s, handwritten news sheets (now

better known as gazettes) were circulated among the people. As I am sure you can imagine, that was very laborious work, but it contained useful information on what was happening around Europe from wars to politics. In 1609, the first printed newspapers were circulated around Germany. There was a lot of censorship on the news at the time, and these newspapers were only allowed to print stories about foreign news. The circulation of newspapers only really began to gain traction in around the 1800s as high speed printing presses began work on newspapers and they became cheaper and faster to produce.

Throughout the later years, massive printing presses began popping up in every town, covering not only foreign news and stories, but also local. Many families would have a daily newspaper delivered to their door every morning. Newspapers do not only hold news and current affairs, but letters from readers, classified ads, and business advertisements which are one of the main sources of income for news houses. Many people feel that, in our day and age of technology and instant information, that newspapers no longer have a place. Judging from the statistics, this might not be true just yet as the estimated total U.S. daily newspaper circulation (print and digital combined) in 2018 was 28.6 million for weekday and 30.8 million for Sunday (Journalism.org). There is a decline year on year, but there are still vast numbers of people consuming news in this fashion, especially in third world and developing countries, where technological coverage is not quite up to par with the rest of the world.

Journalism has come a long way from the days of the first German newspapers and the censorship that was imposed on them. There is a principle called "freedom of the press" in place now whereby communication and expression through various media is a right to be exercised freely. Constitutionally, this stops governments in particular from issuing "gag" orders to members of the press [with the possible exclusion being state security]. This is why there are still people reading newspapers today from reputable news houses. When a news house develops a reputation for delivering accurate researched news to the public, they create a trust between them and the people that the news on which they report is the truth. We read newspapers for an in depth investigation into matters which occur in the world whether it is foreign or domestic.

Speed Reading and Newspapers

The general layout of a newspaper is for each article to be placed in a column format. This was not originally because it was easier to read shorter lines of text, but because of the way the type face was set out in large printing presses. It does make sense, however, that the popularity of newspapers grew because it was almost like taking the news and breaking it down into "bite sized" pieces of information. If you can imagine a newspaper article in a paragraph format over the size of the page, you can understand why the column format also looked better and worked better for the average reader. Newspaper columns are also much better suited to speed reading. If you think back on the lesson on saccades and eye fixation points, you can see that you would need far less fixation points on a column than you would on a traditional paragraph. It's also easier not to allow your eyes to regress as they are moving rapidly over a smaller section of text rather than a chunk of words that they may get lost in.

Let us look at an example of text from "The Outsiders" by S E Hinton in a paragraph format and the same text in columns:

Paragraph:

Suddenly it wasn't only a personal thing to me. I could picture hundreds of boys living on the wrong sides of cities, boys with black eyes who jumped at their own shadows. Hundreds of boys who maybe watched sunsets and looked at the stars and ached for something better. I could see boys going down under street lights because they were mean and tough and hated the world, and it was too late to tell them there was still good in it...There should be some help, someone to tell them before it was too late. Someone should tell their side of the story, and maybe people would understand then and wouldn't be so quick to judge a boy by the amount of hair oil he wore.

Columns:

Suddenly it wasn't only a personal thing to me. I could picture hundreds of boys living on the wrong sides of cities, boys with black eyes who jumped at their own shadows. Hundreds of boys who maybe watched sunsets and looked at the stars and ached for something better.

I could see boys going down under street lights because they were mean and tough and hated the world, and it was too late to tell them there was still good in it...There should be some help, someone to tell them before it was too late.

Someone should tell their side of the story, and maybe people would understand then and wouldn't be so quick to judge a boy by the amount of hair oil he wore.

You should be able to notice that the second copy of that text is a much faster read - your eyes should only be fixating once or at the most twice per line. Saccades are also smoother and if you had to work out your reading speed on the piece, it would be much faster and you would have retained more information by simply using the eye movement techniques and minimizing your subvocalization

Chapter 7: Popular Science Books and Magazines

Possibly the biggest advantage that science books and magazines have over other forms of written media is the inclusion of visual illustrations and examples, something we know already helps improve your memory and information retention. One thing to remember about this media is that there will still be a lot of examples and anecdotes, not all of which will help you to gain information. Popular science books and magazines are critical not only for students who are learning new subjects, but also for those on various career paths who wish to further their knowledge and learn more about the technology and science in their field and for those of us who wish to just consume information about a variety of subjects.

Popular science books and magazines open our perception of the world to new and interesting topics, whether it be actual science, psychology, neurosciences and how the human body works, or technological marvels and how the world around us is changing. We read these books and magazines to get input from various leaders in the different fields of study, to see what new research there is about a variety of topics and to learn more about ourselves and the world around us.

Speed Reading and Popular Science Books and Magazines

As stated earlier, a point to remember about this written medium is that although the facts and science involved may seem really intimidating (especially if you are reading for your own enjoyment), a lot of the text is filled with examples and applications.

Skim reading through these sections is the best approach as you could find a valuable tidbit here and there, then pay more attention to it and absorb that information.

Remember to minimize subvocalization as much as possible as your brain may get stuck on trying to pronounce the more complicated scientific words. If you don't understand them, come back to then at a later stage.

Chapter 8: Instruction Manuals

As we have recounted, today it is extremely important to be able to stay at the top of your field so that you may excel in your respective career. With more and more machinery and software in our work lives, we need to be able to effectively work and maintain it. It is not just at work where we need to read informational leaflets or instruction manuals. Most of our daily lives are now consumed with automated systems and machinery that should, in theory, make our lives better. Then again, when we do not know how to operate it efficiently, it can become frustrating and more of a chore than anything else. Instructional manuals take all of the information that we should know about the software and machinery and how to put things together and present them in a concise easy to navigate format. They usually contain pictures as well as instructions in a booklet form. Instructional books, like this one, tend to give you small bits of information at a time. to help you with going through the steps. These are laid out in chapter form with instructions on how to learn a new skill or subject.

Speed Reading and Instructional Manuals

Because of the nature of an instructional manual, it is easy to speed read through one. Like newspaper articles, most instructional manuals are typed in a column format with short easy to consume sentences.

To best utilize your lessons when attempting to read through an instructional manual, you should use the visualization process.

Because the pictures are usually available for you to look at for each instruction, try to memorize the way the picture shows you how to complete each task.

If there are no pictures available, use your memory training and visualize your own pictures of the instructions.

You can also make use of a memory palace for instructional manuals. Picture each step as you move through the palace and make a note of how what step happens next.

In the case of books, reading through the content page first then visualizing how you are going to get through the information, why you need the information, and taking the time between every subsection to think about how and why it applies to you will help you to absorb that information.

Chapter 9: Fiction

For many of us, taking a good book, putting our feet up, and getting lost in a story is an excellent way to relax and recover from a long day. Novels are a great way to close ourselves off from the world and join an imaginary one be it just someone else's life or a fictional magical world that we transport ourselves into. It's an escape from our reality.

Most people who find themselves reading novels do so to expand their vocabulary, gain greater experience through the writing of others, or simply for the sheer enjoyment. Novels can give us thrill rides and fast paced action, sci-fi journeys to other worlds, or romantic dreams of everything always working out the way it should be.

Reading is good for our mental health. It helps us connect with a world outside our own as well as creating feelings of empathy toward others. Reading also expands our views and helps us to keep an open mind to those around us and situations outside of ourselves and to be more rational as we encounter our own problems. It can also foster more creativity in us as we allow the outside world in, allowing us to come up with interesting solutions to problems we may encounter. Humans constantly seek to identify themselves with others and reading stories of those who may look like us or find themselves in similar situations to us helps us to believe that we too can do great things and conquer life problems. Activities like reading also help to stimulate the brain and are thought to help prevent degeneration in the brain, a cause of dementia. Research has shown that as we read, the brain is engaged. The complex neurons and circuits fire all over, and as we mature in our reading ability, so our brain grows and strengthens. We also learn new vocabulary as we read more, increasing our ability to communicate more effectively so that we are understood better by others.

For some of us, the process becomes frustrating and aggravating because we let things like regression steal time and energy from us as we read. Or, perhaps you are a student who is reading prescribed reading material from your lessons and you find that the book is not catching your attention. These things can become tedious and rob us of the enjoyment that we gain from reading as well as the psychological benefits of reading. How do we get past these issues and find enjoyment and stimulation from reading?

Speed Reading and Fiction

With novels, we can start right at the beginning. Novels are the place that your regressive reading habits will show up the most as they are usually thick paragraphs of text and it is easy for your eyes to wander. Start off by using the lessons you have learned in chapter 1 to resist the regression. This will ease some of the frustration of re-reading sentences for no apparent reason. Most novels will be full of sections that set the scene and describe things and characters. These are not always essential to your comprehension or knowledge when you are reading a novel and if you force yourself to keep reading forward, you will not miss any valuable information.

Subvocalization will rob you of time while you are reading a novel. Try to minimize this as much as possible or you will be reading at the speed that you would normally speak, and this is too slow for speed reading.

When reading a novel, be sure to control your fixation points. These are essential to work with your eye movements to make reading through the paragraphs faster. Make sure to focus your first fixation point about 3 words from the beginning of the line and the last fixation point about 3 words from the end. Try to imagine that the margins are really bad and you don't want to look at them for added incentive. Ideally, you should only have no more than one more fixation point in the middle of the line, but if at the beginning it is difficult, make two fixation points in the center of the line and build up to having only one.

After each chapter, take a few minutes to reflect on what you have read. What characters did you meet? What shape is the story taking? How do you feel about the characters and the circumstances that you read about? Try to picture how the characters look in our head and possibly the locations that you read about. These techniques will help you to remember the story as you progress through it chapter by chapter.

Conclusion

Reading is one of humanity's most treasured possessions.

Most of us need to read some form of text during our day. Students, lecturers, executives, managers, etc. as well as those who read for pleasure or to catch up on the news. Sadly, modern lifestyles and our busy lives demand that everything is on fast forward including what we do in our private lives to relax. We need to run faster if we go for a jog, cook faster, play games better and even read faster than we normally would. This is why speed reading is so beneficial to our lives. Not only do we learn to read faster, but we also learn to process information more efficiently, ensuring that we gain the maximum amount of knowledge from text that we can.

Reading has so many rich benefits to our lives. Not only does it relax us in a way that keeps our brains stimulated and healthy, but it gives us self-confidence, builds our communication and interpersonal skills, and teaches us new things daily. If we wasted time while reading or [heaven forbid] gave it up because we became frustrated and disillusioned at the time it takes to read through and absorb a body of text, we would be missing out on all the wonderful things that reading can do for us.

As humans, we need to constantly be evolving and growing

or we become stuck in a rut in life. Not only will our skills never improve, but we will be faced with an inherent boredom that will start to creep into our lives. When we become bored, we start to lose interest in the people around us and our surroundings. Our work becomes a labor. Our relationships start to feel claustrophobic. Our lives start to feel the same day in and day out. Speed reading is not only a skill that we can learn to boost our self-confidence and take back some of the time we spend poring over text every day, but it is also a skill that unlocks other potential in our lives. When we can use this skill to unlock our ability to learn and grow in other areas of our life, it becomes essential to our personal freedom and happiness.

We hope that you have learned many things while reading this book. Many of these skills, especially for memory, can be used in other aspects of your life as well. We wish you all the best as you journey out into the world of reading with a fresh new perspective and the hunger to learn faster and more efficiently.

Happy Speed Reading!

References

Benefits of Reading. (2019, October 2). SACAP. https://www.sacap.edu.za/blog/applied-psychology/benefits-of-reading

Berg, H. S. (2014, January 24). Why Do We Read So Slowly? How To Learn. https://www.howtolearn.com/2014/01/why-do-we-read-so-slowly/

Chegg.com. (n.d.). How to Improve Memory for Studying in 27 Ways. Chegg. Retrieved August 19, 2020, from https://www.chegg.com/study-101/improve-memory-studying/

Hammond, C. (2019, December 2). Speed reading can seem like an almost superhuman feat – but is it really possible to read quickly and retain the information? BBC. https://www.bbc.com/future/article/20191129-how-to-learn-to-speed-read

Moats, L., & Tolman, C. (2016, May 5). Eye Movements and Reading. Reading Rockets. https://www.readingrockets.org/article/eye-movements-and-reading

Mohs, R. C. (n.d.). How Human Memory Works. How Stuff Works. Retrieved August 19, 2020, from https://science.howstuffworks.com/life/inside-the-mind/human-brain/human-memory2.htm

Nowak, P. (2014, December 29). Speed Reading Tops - 5 Ways to Minimize Subvocalization. Iris Reading. https://irisreading.com/speed-reading-tips-5-ways-to-minimize-subvocalization/

Rodrigues, J. (2011, July 26). 5 Reasons Why Speed Reading Is Good For Your Brain. Iris Reading. https://irisreading.com/5-reasons-why-speed-reading-is-good-for-your-brain/

Spreeder. (2010a, July 31). Learn to Speed Read by Expanding Your Field of Vision. https://www.spreeder.com/learn-to-speed-read-by-expanding-your-field-of-vision/

Spreeder. (2010b, August 7). Learn To Read Faster - Stop Regressing. https://www.spreeder.com/learn-to-read-faster-stop-regressing/

Sutz, R., & Weverka, P. (n.d.). Eye Exercises for Speed Reading. Dummies. Retrieved August 18, 2020, from https://www.dummies.com/education/language-arts/speed-reading/eye-exercises-for-speed-reading/

T, R. (2014, December 8). Avoid Regression - Speed Reading. Insanity Mind. http://www.insanity-mind.com/avoid-regression-speed-reading/

The Mind Tools Content Team. (n.d.). Speed Reading. Mind Tools. Retrieved August 16, 2020, from https://www.mindtools.com/speedrd.html

White, R. (2015, December 15). Calculate Reading Speed - Speed Reading Tips and Hints. Memorise. https://memorise.org/speed-reading/calculate-reading-speed

Wikipedia. (2003, November 25). Speed Reading. https://en.wikipedia.org/wiki/Speed_reading

Wikipedia. (2006a, April 10). History of Newspaper Publishing. https://en.wikipedia.org/wiki/History_of_newspaper_publishing

Wikipedia. (2006b, November 26). Eye Movements in Reading. https://en.wikipedia.org/wiki/Eye_movement_in_reading

Wikipedia. (2006c, November 26). Fixation (Visual). https://en.wikipedia.org/wiki/Fixation_(visual)

Made in the USA
Middletown, DE
31 October 2020

23092076R00057